Advanced Praise for *Blood Women*

"Blood runs through this poignant collection, as lifeforce, as a biological fluid, and as an emblem for love.

There is reverence here, for the women in the poet's life, and compassion. He meditates about his daughters, about familial blood ties and the mystery of heredity, the 'spirals of life congealed in /my blood'. Memories of intense joy are mixed with grief. 'My heart is gapped'.

Behind all the poems lie the keen sensibilities of a scientist who sees more than most of us in our everyday physicality. 'Blood has universes inside its skin,/ codes and expressions of us.' Lyricism comes clad in scientific terms. When the poet as a child sees his mother smile, he exclaims, 'I knew she was my calcium.' Through his stark and tender poetry, Stephen Paul Wren unravels the mystical truths of our biochemistry, and our humanity."

- Lesley Curwen, author of *Rescue Lines*, Hedgehog Poetry Press

"Stephen Paul Wren is quickly becoming one of my favourite contemporary poets, not only for his linguistic inventiveness that pairs science with soul, using technical terms to illuminate the art found in every atom, but also for his tenderness. *Blood Women* is an exquisite example of Wren's beautiful vulnerability, and his choice to use his talents to revere the women in his life is a moving, exceptional triumph. These poems also bite, bringing everything back to blood and all it symbolises - the sacrifice of birth and menses, of danger and violence, of caring for wounds, and the gentle, sometimes heartbreaking reminder that Wren's own blood is part of the legacy of the women before him, and those who come after. I cannot recommend *Blood Women* enough."

-Briony Collins, author of *Ambergris*, Barnard Publishing LTD

Blood Women

Blood Women

Stephen Paul Wren

PARLYAREE
PRESS

Parlyaree Press
Atlanta, Georgia
www.parlyaree.com

Copyright © 2025 by Stephen Paul Wren
All Rights Reserved
Printed locally; distributed globally
First Edition, 2025

Library of Congress Cataloging-in-Publication Data
Names: Wren, Stephen Paul, author.
Title: Blood Women / Stephen Paul Wren
Description: First Edition | Atlanta : Parlyaree Press, 2025
Identifiers: LCCN: applied for | ISBN 9781961206250 (paperback)
Subjects: LCGFT: Poetry
LC record available at https://lccn.loc.gov/

Interior & Cover Design by Parlyaree Press

Typeset in Hightower. Cover and Interior Imagery Licensed for use.

Print ISBN: 978-1-961206-25-0
Ebook ISBN: 978-1-961206-26-7

For my blood mother,
blood daughters (real and imaginary),
a blood grandmother,
and other women.

Blood Women

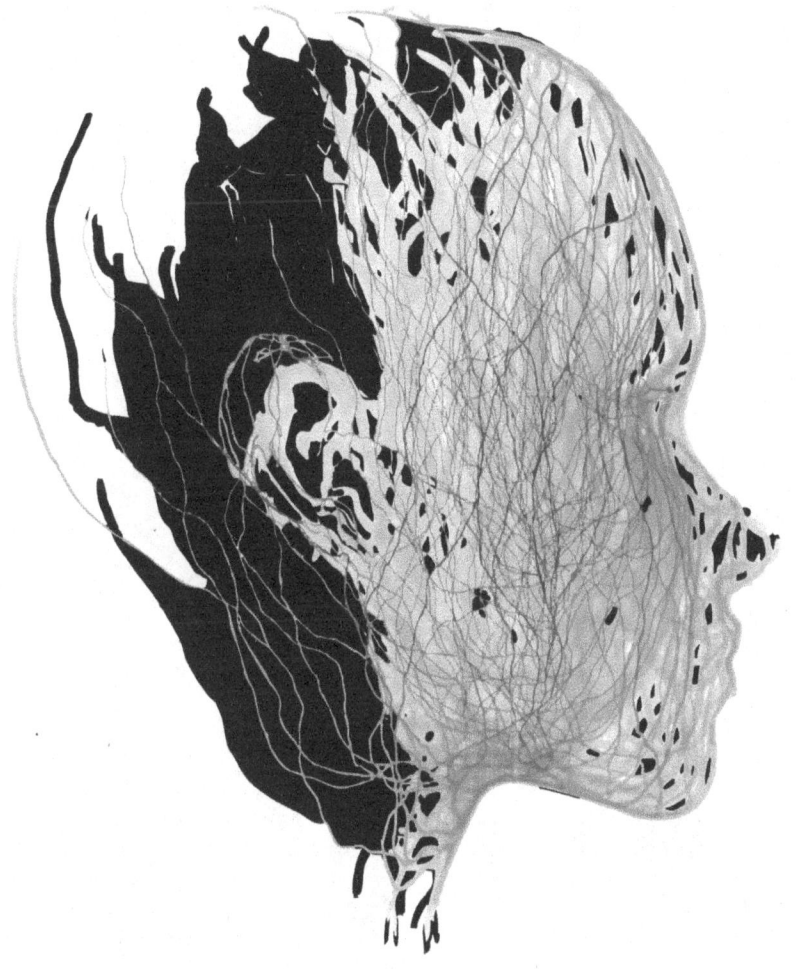

Stephen Paul Wren

TABLE OF CONTENTS

A flood of blood

(i)

The Earth is bleeding out
What is the secretion?
Whatever the motif,
the blood women are swimming in my head.
In vessels.
Like comfortable itches.

(ii)

One of the women is my daughter.
(praying for balancing of hormones etc)

(iii)

The woman formed by a hypothetical fertilisation is beautiful.

(iv)

It started with a flood of blood.
Perhaps, it finished there too?
A home. A bosom of blood.
Where all the building blocks of my life snapped into position.
Where fountains of aged youth gush.

Heredity

I watch the girl with custard coloured hair
Disappear between the bollards. I am
Fifty yards away. This is our walk home
From junior school. A blunt dog scares me.
I enter the road that completes the trip
My family made from working class to
Upper middle. An entropic twitch shocks
Me. Two daughters are given to me. My
Inheritance is their inheritance.
Do I see the patterns? Recurring frosts.
Those forsaken nucleotides. Phosphates
To remember and cherish. I walk by
Churchyard graves and notice something beneath
The warm air. Spirals of life congealed in
My blood. I ask *What is heredity?*

The light of day

Hums. An imperfect register.
My daughter's music (her presence) plays in her yellow room.
My mind still hears the rush of excitement before her birth.
So many jobs.
Walls to paint with sun. I recall the art's sleeve.
Head near hot lightbulb.
My Eiffel Tower stepladder. Brushed light.
She does not see my tears
as I leave the house. The family splits.
Now she is gone.
She waits for me through the crystals of Heaven.
Sits by a still shore. A lake sleeps.
Her log cabin's walls are yellow.
Reflections from her face of sun.

Pocahontas

I felt the finished work of Joy when she
sang the song from *Pocahontas*. Balance
was seen as the open canoe cut through
still water on our television screen.
You can paint with all the colours of the
wind. An obtuse block of stars gave me light.

Mirrows of dew

She jumps and skips.
Choose a biome for her.

She runs and climbs.
Urge green pigments to faint.

Small hurdles seethe.
Over loams (they renew).

She wins each race.
Soils fix their hydration.

Her dad applauds.
The terrain suits ankles.

Mirrors of dew.
Capture her businesses.

Her glow goes out.
Air still hangs orange there.

Her purviews grow.
Animals breathe in fields.

Human absence.
A vacuum after sports.

I mould brain stems.
Searching for the start line.

I cling to trees.
For they perceive true lights.

My heart is gapped.
To fathom this is hard.

She wins again.
Earth itself vanishes.

She is Mother's skin.
Daughter of nature's day.

Life demands more.
More than cleaning sunsets.

Blood

Blood is a curtain containing iron,
but is best described as a source of life.
Perhaps the slight origin of us all.
Blood has universes inside its skin.
Codes and expressions of us. The substance
is more joyous than birthday cake icing.
Blood is an equal of water. In the
Stockholm Archipelago there is a
a harbour where the boats are cells. Baltic
Seawater is gone. It's replaced by blood.
I see people on the quayside, but where
is my daughter? Somewhere better. Somewhere
with no bad temper. Washes of blood pass
over our blood. Does it hurt us? Looking
out at the wash created by a cruise
ship, I see a nut, hard and small, brittle
on the inside (probably). Intense.
The answer to fixing my disorder
is self-centred (like the nature of its
behaviour). Is my hope a whisper
in my blood? Can a soul be bottled up
in sea glass, or in flasks of burly flesh?

Arc

We gazed at the stairs. We were in the arc.
Stress charged the outer rims of my body.

Rushes of blood were checked by excitement.
My two daughters ran up the final few steps.

Their phones spun into concentricity.
On top, cityscape photos were taken;

Lights, shadows, and minitutae. Timelapsed.
When they took selfies, I fought vertigo.

The girls flocked with the birds. Safari souls.
I descended to a lower deck. Rapt.

We paraded down the Champs-Élysées,
In a dream, as if we were royalty.

Somewhere in my blood I felt the truth speak.
We were just like all the other tourists.

Pupa

walking with you
late afternoon
green on our left
fence on our right
warm air at work
moving your hair
tanning your skin

through a prism
larval structures
break down for good
a hormone set
controls the growth
of adult forms

planning our trip
to my uncle's
and his music
(he fiddles well)
we start to dance
along the path
our lives mending

why do outbreaks
from safe places
hurt like frostbite?
I see goodwill
watching the scene
with shouts and purrs

(the impact of
divorce is gone)
we might be free
in this pupa
we laugh loudly
we don't yet know
days like this pass

the outside world
splits into view
chewing the skin
to soften silk
this kind elbow
reveals our wings

Fists

Our fists side-by-side, palm-side down,
(four squares with turrets for knuckles),
remind me of our overlapping genes.
Your fists are perfect square,
adipose-smooth.
My fists are more imperfect,
scored with blue veins.
The similarity of our fists, though, is clear.
I want to see your DNA, learn its sequences,
immerse myself in its aqueous order.
So, I look at your fists.
So, that I can remember you
(the biological you)
on days when you are not physically here.
But, heavy cloud surrounds me, a delightful corpus.
There is so much more to you than fists.
Climbing out of your biology,
your nucleotides,
is your soul and, concurrently, your soul envelops your cells.
Your soul is beautiful,
gentle like Clementia.
Your fists don't throw punches,
they are only memorials to your existence here,
the merest heat
becoming parcels of love.
Our fists side-by-side, palm-side down,
our moment in time,
on Earth. Unearthing identity.

Blood groups

<u>A</u> (red blood cells with antigen A)

A mother calling her son in for tea.
After my day of playing football and cricket on a village green.

or

Ashen women of every kind.

<u>B</u> (red blood cells with antigen B)

Blackbirds pecking the grass on a village green.
Batallions of them.

or

Browbeaten women trying to wrestle some control back in their
lives.

<u>AB</u> (red blood cells with both antigen A and B)

A mother who is abreast of everything.
Banal tasks whipped into a frenzy of joy.

or

Alert women gifted in ways the world never gets to hear about.
Bright women with blusher on.

<u>O</u> (red blood cells with neither antigen A or B)

Onwards she goes. A mother preparing food and thinking for her family.

or

Outrageous inequality. Opportunities lost.

Rhesus factor

Rhesus positive is the glow that a son feels for his mother. He goes home with an inherited protein located on the surface of his red blood cells.

Rhesus negative is the anger felt on the wrong end of control. Like a lack of protein in blood.

Gold medal

Mum wore a bright dress that day.
Her tensile hair moved in the sea breeze.
Her brown sweater proved to be an effective barrier against the
rising wind.

She smiled at the camera.
I knew she was my calcium;
for, by those Cornwall cliffs,
my health was preserved by her toils.
That was her Nobel Prize.
Her gold medal.
Her motherhood.
Her untiring ability to nurture,
to correct my brother and I,
with more tools at her disposal than the number of sand particles
all around us.

On that beach, I understood a new, sharper definition of love.

We were unaware of the iron core way below us
and our sandcastles.
With a resolute hardness
at the centre of the Earth, a dry magnetic field protected us from
the sun's glare.
We were unmoved by its static.

It almost felt that Mum had a role in all this.
Did she impact the non-accidental gears of the world?
Did she play in the orchestra of God?

Photographic paper recorded her eyes for me.
I was more blessed than the merciful.

Daffodils

Benevolent hydra, all heads yellow,
catch the light on the windowsill, drink it,
share it with your angled arms and green flesh,
your fresh lichen, your show of ancient art.

Offer yourself to my departed mum,
she walks the Earth again, balancing song
with placental support, her cloth of love
mapped out, covering ruffled air, my blood.

Decorate a field with a flash of gold,
the sun stills, soil acidity is low.
How do you sense the ground's level of lime?
Do you settle into the role of Hope?

Grace my hospital room, I stand, so young,
groggy and sore, mum says *turn on the tap,
it helps you wee*, the antiseptic gauze
is moved back, I limp towards the flowers.

Joy of orbits
do not depart
Doctors of note
draw out bad blood
So, look deeper
for benign cells
Keep her soul here

bad blood is lank
I shun the trade
just drain off blood

lood

rth tilt
s room
 world
sons
rkers
od
ife

 rich
ours
 blood

and bake the sun
it is too soon
and sickly skins
bad blood is still red
swap the cancer
let the light in
then it hit me

it hangs around
too big a price?
leave us alone

Barely audible

Mum's mum worked at a
biscuit factory.
I did not eat treats
with her; Time acted
like bubonic light.
Stopped us sharing life.
Dried the slide of tea.
Kept our hands apart.

Mum's mum's pink colour
made photos richer.
Haywire cells lived
beneath the surface
of her skin, and prints
with a matte finish.
I found a birthday
card written by her.

Mum's mum had a voice
imbued with a harp.
Unique crashes, soft
to the touch, distant,
vitreous, and near.
I tried to hear it
through the muzzle of youth.
What was that movement?

More than one meniscus

A smell of blood - droplets that stain - essences of womenhood
(that touch my life) carried -
dismembering my abdication - I am shocked into remembrance -

these ladies are absorbers of shock - carpels that clothe from a
distance -
stigmas that snatch protective pollen at close quarters -
stabilisers of my joints - I adore this salient cartography.

Meniscus one,

is there a mythology for the failing body?
Norse?
Greek?
Machine-to-tomb-to-curiosity. In the blink of an eye.

Grasping the image of your eyes, I want to swim in their
atmospheres.
Breathe in sea.

Blue, or not blue,
The tricks of light connect to your last breath.

An embolus gathers all its terrible moss.
A descent that would fascinate you.
A case study in your medical student notes.
A wrecking ball that tilts your life's balance.

Yet, I learn so much from you.

Meniscus two,

blood appears in your knee joint.
Despite this,
you wear the overcoat of God.

Your bravery and focus inspire me so much that my meniscus
does not tear.
You stop blood entering my joint.

Meniscus three,

Be yourself you say.
I thank you for that.

You are bleeding from tumour vasculatures.
Your blueprint for walking here keeps me smiling.

Meniscus four,

you bequeath the king of kings.
You make me read a new thesis of love.

I see you swim beneath a rectangle of sky.
You splash
and the sun bites its temper.

Your strength cuts through salt.

Here, I fumble deep deep in gratitude.
I run with awareness and healthy knees.

Beneath my skin is an ocean of blood.
Its sticky grip now loose as I hear trees.

Yes, hear.
There are also movements of air.
More than one meniscus sings in the breeze.

Some poems in this collection have appeared in the following publications:

The Light of Day - *14 Magazine*

Mirrors of Dew - *Black Cat Poetry Press Anthology*

Gold Medal - *Shine*

Bad Blood - *Lothlorien Journal*

Pupa - *Obsessed with Pipework*

Fist - *Life's Wonder's Anthology*, Black Bear Press

Founded in Atlanta, Georgia in 2023, PARLYAREE PRESS is dedicated to publishing writing that expands, reveals, and interrogates the mainstream. We seek out fiction, creative nonfiction, and poetry that exists in the liminal space between what was and what will be.

The cant of circus performers, freaks, queers, and thespians, Parlyaree is the invented language required to tell the stories of those othered, to keep their secrets, to keep them safe. It is a polyglot of experiences that may only be told in one's own voice. Parlyaree—as an invented language—borrows from what was to create something new.

That is what excites us at Parlyaree Press. Stories that transform; essays that reimagine; poetry that takes us behind the stanza to the core of our being and back again; language that plays as much as it conveys.

Writers: tell us your secrets.
Readers: reimagine your worlds.